*Thank you to all my listeners, especially
to Helen, Jane and Norman.   E.B.*

Cover design by CheckPoint Press from an original idea by John
Ward, with grateful acknowledgement to Julius Guzy for the use of
his acrylic painting (image inserted)
"Looking through the branches of a weeping willow"
www.juliuspaintings.co.uk

Looking
Down
Through
Water

Elizabeth Bazeley

CheckPoint
Press

Looking Down Through Water

ISBN: 978-1-906628-08-6

Published by CheckPoint Press, Ireland

CHECKPOINT PRESS, DOOAGH, ACHILL ISLAND, CO. MAYO,
REPUBLIC OF IRELAND
TEL: 098 43779
EMAIL: EDITOR@CHECKPOINTPRESS.COM

WEBSITE: WWW.CHECKPOINTPRESS.COM

To the memory of
Margaret Carpenter

CONTENTS

. . .   it was she
who vainly tried to pull
pieces of fuselage from the silt
as though to reconstruct her world

but they only sank deeper . . .

PAINTING THE BEACH

A wash of sunlight too dazzling for
wide-open eyes
Whiteness
which slowly streaks and drifts
subtle   pastel
and separates into hues
Amorphous
vistas elongating luminous
mauve-teal parquetry
taupe
saffron
sage green
brushed through
palest flaxen
Chance figurines (the rovers and paddlers
the children the dogs)
imposing minute perspective
a near impossibility
in such far distances
Airy ambiguous blue
condensing with nacreous nuance
to caverns and castles
of purple and rose . . .

Too evanescent even for the fluidity of colour,
never mind for the honesty of a dream maker.

INTERFACE: a curlew

Wavening watery silver
                silvery aqua swirling
        the moorings, shushening the sand.
    Shorebirds, a shellpicker
                patient and hungry
            follow the tide froth
            back   forth
    gleaning the line of the homegoing sea.

Listen.

    They listen, the shellpicker, the shorebirds
                        somewhere beyond
            out where the sea goes to meet
                palely pearly
                the sky's dissolution
    somewhere bewailing
                    loss in an emptiness
        close as a shoulder (the shellpicker turns)
                the marsh or the shallows

        now silent   invisible   and again
            eerie   (they hear it)

            a fugitive's call
            an outlaw's lament
            to shorebirds a brother
            to the shellpicker ghostly . . .

12

Be still.   Surely
        the hidden cry
                                - ringing -
              to haunt you it echoes from
                                further beyond.
            Hushen the wavening water and still
                        the back and forth swings
                of the white frilly froth.

    Who knows if it's empty
                                that sky
                or inhabited.

The birds peck their prey
                        while the shellpicker pauses
                mystified   wondering
                        what calls beyond.
Surely the emptiness echoes a secret . . .

What appears vaporous
                            here meeting there
                shimmery fearsomeness surely

                    - just listen -

The shorebirds rise as one wing
                                wheel away
                out somewhere beyond
        palely . . .

13

FROSTY DAWN

The lawn of white brocade.
         Pearly hedge.
Rimed roofs
         (altars with candelabra of chimneys)
rosied by rays preceding the sun
         over the first rim of the morning.
Choirs of curious excited birds
         fly airy tracery.

From the rim at my window of morning
         incantations precede me onto the day
                  over
the sill, a weaving there of sea shades, charm-strewn
         (restored shore of shells and stones) with
a spray of wild grasses captured in a vase
         of frosted glass traced
in designs intrinsic as forever.

Were the predecessors
         to cross dark ledges of the years,
patterning the blood more indelibly
         with joy than remorse,
cutting sacred runes less sorrowfully
         deep into the bones of the progeny,
would there need be supplication
         for the grace of frost's ephemerae?

TIDAL POND IN WINTER

Ice-still.

The golden grasses framing
as lashes do
a blind black eye.
There are secrets
in that eye.
I watched you drop them in
that love-grey time
you thought them mired
like sunken ships,
cracked hulls of hopes,
the offerings of heart-melt.
I hear you
wish them back
but they are refracted
in onyx.

Softly now the day
warms, edges come away.
A silvery eye
reflects your empty sigh
as you wait the cycle through of hours
for it to yield its insights

- until the silver I
(sallying up the sky)
cast my sidelong smile
into the symbiotic pool, its guile
retrieves my vanity but not your lone desire.
How were you to know you'd found
the hand mirror of the moon
in her vast boudoir?

WORSHIPPING TREES

There
a twisted crone
with winter flying out of her fingers
and the moon rising in her hair

and here standing folk
joined at the heartbeat
jettison their cries which hang like frosted hawks
before riding the wind away.

Her broken twigs divine the springs
where hopeful offerings of corn and apples are laid,
her fallen branches burn courageous outposts
into the cold night.
                    Firelight
dances with dancers,
leaping legs, flickering feet,
and dispatches flame-feathered messages
to gods in the dark

until silence.

And silence until
up there along the ridge
a sigh stirs the watchful grey giants
appearing like magicians in the dawning clarity
and the chilled crone
waits to warm herself at the hearth.
Facing eastward to catch the sun on their great limbs
they draw the first rose-gold breath of day
and embrace humbly the children of earth.

But the old old
gnarled Mother with forks of magic
divines the eternal fountain of Spring
and softly readies in new green
                              again
the sun's leafy bride

while earth's children,
who long for perpetual dress and fountains everlasting
are tearing the wood apart limb from limb and
leaving sacred fires untended and
pouring away the last eternity

until the breath of light
ignites the trees.

When the forest is in smoking ruin
only a longing child will watch for a cross to leaf.

```
            IO
RE      T  NS
      FLEC
      FLEC
RE      CT NS
   E      C IO S
```

Greened as ancient bronze
is water where drowned
dancers are caught
in slender white tranquil poses

birds flutter through their fingers
as if just their jewellery is not stilled
and floating flowers like candles guide
their feet into deeper secrets

while you pause amid the irises
with fish in your hair
like a statue on a pavilion.

A wind walks over the surface
                              dividing us
by a texture. By awareness.

The dancers bent in a bough of grace
break quivering
and the candles flicker out
and birds slip behind the foliage
into secrets I do not understand.

Though you may

for it is I you see amid irises
waterlight bronzing my hair
and casting its wavery replica over the leaves
and its dances round the still white birches

you slip into secrets behind time
leaving only your shimmer
as irises furled on the brink
are netted in flight between worlds.

Were I not caught like the dancers
drowned in their grace
I would follow the candles placed for my feet.
Instead I am set as though shimmer were stone
reflected through a texture,
believing I am stamped with a singular truth.

BORDERLANDS

We circle the planet
prowling from day to day
crossing the starfields.
At dusk we crouch on our hunches
prospecting, keeping watch
for the signal to rekindle on the mountain,
a glacier to flash diurnal cipher,
or waiting to see if the rains
                will part their silver curtains
again and ever again.
It is there, the promise, the fable,
a sapphire glistens and beckons
                in its swirl of filigree.

There are no eyes to see us,
it is we who would bring the power of vision.
In silence like smoke we go unheard
for only we would become listeners.
In this dimension being is
                merely
our circling wraiths longing
to thirst for milk in the throat,
to desire the body's honey fragrance.
Scrawled across the surface our nomadic shadows
(which will one day startle and delight you with theory)
search for our place, our stopping,
                enfoldment for our flocks.

We are time, we are law, we are will,
able to fashion ourselves from the morphogenetic navel
and take root to grow like trees
in wise orchards.
It is with consensus that we may proceed.
We are not thieves.

*

Circling the heart now
scouting through an outrageous darkness
I hear the beat and discern
in a lighted window in the wall
a shape, a desire
which touched might yield
    the pleasures of silk
        the chastity of petals
            or the store of sun in the rock.

Wasn't it promised, isn't it mine?

        The drum is summons
meaningless without my knowledge,
pulsating a perpetual question
which unanswered is my demon.

I will break in
and with the squads of time
run heavy-booted through the lanes,
pitch torches into sleeping chambers,
clamber across gardens
        churning their scent into the wallows,
rattle locked doors 'til they give
        - and the drummer is found -
And so drag off my rightful joy.

*

When you are glimpsed through the lattice
among the leaves and fruit of your mosaic shrine
you magnify the sun until our hearts catch fire.
Silhouetted in a pool of twilight
you bring down the stars
as easily as our promises
to be your eternal gardeners.

Though we long for your blessing
you are a stillness reflecting.
Though we request an oracle
you are mutely knowing
that we know your structure is our form and light.
And even when we reject your purity
we claim you for our ancestor and god
carried from paradise in chains.

The outer rages burn now inside the wall
closer until
the drummer stops and hears the crackling dead.
While in your shrine your image melts
into pools reflecting smoke
as brazenly as if you shone there still.
And we, encircled finally, dream
                              dream
            of the wild borders beyond.

SPELLBINDER

Land at rest but breathing
                softly
flushed with the sun
                warm enough
in comfortable seedy grasses

it speaks
           air-tongued
for voices layered
             like choirs
only heard as silence.

If you pass your guardian
                hazes sleeping
to the noise of bees
             you enter
the conspiracy of time and land
                  the keep
of specimens they've plucked
                and pinned
inside our trance
           in amber
cases for display.

Those are your wings
             illuminated
in eternal keep
          the records
clear to read are you
            you are
cloaked in the land
             woven of grasses
through time's warp
            treadled
by the haunting
           humming
of these peculiar days.

23

A breath of presence
                    intersects
the hoops of land
                    the stills of time
a spiral of our knowing
                    joining
all we are
        we were.

THE INHABITANTS

The place was inside the shelter of rock
under the ice sheath
over which had flowed millennia.

Somehow the smoke remained suspended
unmoving in darkness and solid cold
after the fire died
and the ancestors became voices.
Ice carved a glaring green guardian
against air and robbery
until time
        snaking through the ferns
looped and came back.

Recall how you blunder into an abandoned room
where chairs are pushed away from a table,
curtains half-drawn over the light,
cushions imprinted and unplaced, the vase attending -
You know the cake and hyacinths are fresh
and the child has just now stopped singing.
You pause,
        your senses turned to velvet,
before liberating the vanished presence.

An ancient woman alive inside the rock
was suspended in darkness and cold,
twisted out of the smoke like rope,
her features carved by the ice of age
and her eyes deeply burning.
Holding out her hands
which became vivid as they left her captivity
she gave me her legend
to live over and over like chain links
or scar tissue.

25

TOTEM

With and against the wind
my fingertips clinging to yours
we were its two directions both at once
like brothers, like sisters
and butterflies riding the paradox of the current.

We were the same filament of silk
which weaves either side
and touches at our crossing
I with your wisdom, you with my mystery
like teacher and friend, like fire and snow
and wolves in their constancy.

If you have sloughed the pattern we designed
you cannot now mirror my inner snakeside.
If dynamite has tumbled the cliff into the forest
I am unable to send back your echo.
The butterflies are frozen
and no longer come on the wings of returning summer.
I was watching the skies for your whereabouts
when a furred flank brushed past and was gone.

Now I am the experience
of the arriving snows burying the land and its cries,
the thickening pelt and the kill I consume,
the shelter I warm with my breath and blood,
of waiting until I vanish,
waiting until I am forgotten,
waiting
until I know hunger and remember love.

PLUTO PASSING

In those drowsy dappled shallows
flashing with mindfish
skittish with the approach of dreams
you extinguish the lamp.   Instantly
I am at the mouth of your sleep
in my raven's cape.
Night visitors crowd behind me with inquiries
as they peer at you through my feathers.

My lamp aloft replicates yours
with all light extracted as if by miners
or earthworms. So utterly black
the globe absorbs into its collapsing aura both
meaning of your past and vision of your future,
their cords of attachment snapping
as they vanish inward
stranding you without time.

You are my prisoner in a frail dissolving bed.
I am your nihilist.

Yet clasping with sleep-saturated hands
a live counter-orbital swan's egg,
you ignite an oval of flame which
melts its own hollow, becomes a beacon
to signal through the arctic lenses of your heart
until it bursts the sunrise.

Disintegrating from within I thin to shell.

The hatching swan emerges,
unfurls herself and floats like a copper rose
down the waters of the black moon
into a tapestry
woven with the rituals of day

LOSS

Those trees have walked.
And that hill lain down crumpling
the road across its back
into rock formations.
Seasons are doubtful on a flood plain
disciplined by the grim order of the shoreline.
The sun mills vapours into riddles.

Thoughts like disoriented migrants
roost on absent twigs.
A conversation between lovers
once climbing into the privacy of the sky
can now be overheard
distorting itself amid fallen scenery
with delight.
Botanists in the wetlands
are picnicking on store-bought cake
and netting lazy butterflies.

You are gone like a star in the water
when night fades and a weft of dark work
is unfolded by dawn:
trees walking
a hill crumpling
tints of dream awash
                    and you
impermanent as the fragile butterfly
you were chasing yesterday
across its homeland.

AFTER MUSIC

1837

Quayside.
A piper reels out the departing ship
on the last drone stretched
until it breaks into silence
widening with the water.

The notes have fallen like the rain
now stopped, dropped and left
atop the cliff behind the harbour
from where I watch.
Air clears, runnels seep into the moss
and sun paints the hills like a picture
to endure against a wall. The hush
is like a coffin closing.

Compelled down the firth by a sheep-dog wind
the sails grow small.
A plover in pursuit beyond its element
is my winged heart frantic for survival,
to be perched and safely in the rigging,
but it is failing, falling back,
wheeling for the shore
as the ship twists through the veins of sea
red as my own blood against the west.

You told me you would go, my girl.
You told me gently, and I knew so well
hope had deserted us, our place,
our dying land. The young men gone to war
or maybe just a better hope.
Carrying the race we'd reached the last outcrop,
but you must travel further yet, daughter,
and take my spirit like a cup of holy water
past my sacrifice, my death.

Death and sacrifice, what proud words merely.

It was my courage broken when you said
your sister would go too.

There was a night
I rocked a fevered bairn, hearing each tiny gasp,
listening for the next to follow,
accompanied her faltering breath with my even one
as I waited for the melody to end.
                                        Then
I saw an ember in the hearth,
live beneath the ash,
waver newly-roused to flame.
And then I saw the stars
come struggling to the window from the torn sky,
angels hurrying.
She lay like firelight flickering in my arms
until her breathing steadied, sweetened,
and I laid her prayer-wrapped in her cradle.

They've grown strong, I have raised
strong and pleasing daughters. Thus they leave.
When I bade farewell I parted too
from their unborn, never will I hold
nor welcome them until God brings them home
- time and sorrow gone
the way music is gone with the final note.
My anger was more bearable than separation,
bitterness easier than despair, bewilderment
the expression I would last see in their eyes.
It was my heart, wings beating,
hovering between us as they glimpsed themselves
like netted fledglings in my ken.
                                        I turned away
to climb the cliff behind the harbour.

They'll not know I waited
for the melody to end and saw the sails unfurl
against the luring glare of water
or that, so quiet it is
along the walk back to the hills,
all I hear is bees in heather
and a wind sigh in the crags,

behind me sea and silence broadening,
deepening.
   Grief
is the blessing I have sent with them
in bundles darkly stowed, miasma disembarked,
exotic worms for feeding innocents
in pristine nests.

Like chapel walls the hills abide
without compassion, fists on stone
break nothing but my bones.
Yet I watch a painter brushing light
over the timeless heights and into crevices,
altering colour with his whim, reforming
shadow out of weather.

Picture follows picture across days endlessly.
    I listen
to music heard no more.

LILIES GROWING WILD IN THE GARDEN OF LAMENTATION
on learning of a death uncommemorated

Dear ones,
you who are chosen to bear the unbearable,
did you not know when you left me dead
that I was with you
dying in your life?

You believed
the ship's fire charring my flesh
would consume my essence,
your stopped tears would still let the sea wash over me
denying that tears and sea are the same salt,
your grief burying mine over yours
would commit your agony to dust,
and that war swallowed the bones without choking.

I am the dark boy
whose seed eyes multiply as they search your sorrows,
who howls in the wells of your sleep
                    where there are no dreams
only to surface in the visions of the innocent.
Would you have me lick sharp the knife
to cut the harrowed stalk from our shared root
as though the dead could be assigned your rites
as well as your duties?
Unless we make our pact to allow my suffering
its form and time,
yours cannot ripen to love
and I will live wild in your marrow.

Until I return
in the lily's purity
       as its golden heart and white-voiced trumpet
          as the offering of my forgiveness,
remember me in your song
            transmuted, whole, smiling my goodbyes.

THE WIDOWS

Good Friday, 1999

After the massacre

the widows
like thin leafless trees
in the mist the cold
ether of dead men

wait

swaying and keening in a wind
which calls the souls
the dead men
into the arms of the hills

yet wait still
as if there is no choice.
No choice uproots them
they do not file away
along long long
the barren blasted track

until the fear
and cries of children tear them
out of the final
embrace of phantoms

amputations dragged
in disbelief sliced bone
from bone memory
from memory they
follow signs the ancestors
have posted
to indicate directions
for the living.

LOOKING DOWN THROUGH WATER

Depths are shallowed, flattened, darkened with history
    forbidden in stormy seas.
Drowned wives, flooded hearths,
childbirth with no document, record of vandalism
    are gone, but there for any unbeliever.

Creatures of the day, curling in foam
                  golden
    on a wave's green back,
peer down through the dimensions:
translucence over currents and corals,
shifts and shafts of the memory of ourselves,
our source, our wandering,
blue glowing like night lights
left on for us to find a kingdom
belonging to the creatures of an aeon,
purples that probe the layer of a time still indigo
to time's stillness.

The head that casts a shadow in the volcanic lake
sees itself with fish for eyes
and a corona of stars,
              fires which burned
    light years ago
when the crater also held fire.
Two extinct hands clap,
water gives birth to flames,
and creation sips from its image
perpetually.

Like a flood tide sliding its tongue beneath the door
during the storm's lull, lapping at the bottom step,
then the next one,
imperceptibly the water rises around a sleeper
until her bewildered awakening
                                    looking down through dawn,
            her dreams floating.

Trapped in its brass pot a lily
reaches for her fingers,
treadmarks cross floorboards
as if they belonged to refracted ghosts,
eyes watch from that sunken chair
and words from spilled jewellery
remember her.
                        Playing in the stairwell
children smile forever
though meaning bubbles desperately from their mouths
while down in the parlour
a baby swims like a frog.

Looking down through time's deceptive layers
she reflects on herself surrounded by a sunlit window.

SKYLIGHT

scours round the kitchen with its beam
    like a clock hand turning hours to days,
fixates me with its rhomboid eye
    which threatens to punish by enlightenment
even as I am wired to my functional module
    like the clean useful beauty of an appliance.

Although the coffee I am drinking is the bottom of the pot left
    by my son Greg before he set off for work
in a manner reminiscent of the way his father left
    a brew when he set off forever
and the plum jam on my toast is the last of the batch
    my dad made when he was living on his own
and this dwelling was paid for by my second husband
    by the time he died,
I am empty-mouthed.

And then though the noon sun simmers an arrangement
    of grapes and apples, a mango, in nostalgia
tempting me to lunch indecorously from the bowl,
instead of eating them I paint them,
    preserving quickly with the light,
and spite my hunger.

Across the east wall a chestnut branch does shadow tricks,
blooms, leafs, bears, dies, pulling my days around the year
    for amusement. I nibble cheese.
        It's got so late.

Potato steam shrouds twilight
    and the lids clatter like bad-fitting teeth.
How should I know who's dancing in the rafters?
Looking upward for advice I find the sky
    switched off. The stopped clock face
is only mine.

I lied. I lied.

Greg poked his head in the door this morning
    gently to pronounce fresh coffee ready
and I'd intended making chutney from the fruit for Dad
    to spite his nurse who warned spice troubles him.

WRITTEN ON WALLS

You told me you had loved her once.
We were following a frosty sun
supped on winter's lip, delicious
with our confidences.

Hollows filled with clarified twilight,
bubbled with shiny trinket stalls
where we browsed for her, you
wistfully fingering memories.

You bought a graceful samovar,
tessellated, set on flame
unextinguished in the chamber
of your heart.

Then the drinks we stopped for
warmed the aura, sparked our inner tesserae,
a brimming glass displacing
sadness in your eyes.

You took me home, the tea was shared,
candles burned to show me corners
and dispel the shadow from a wall,
revealing words you'd written in lampblack

               like a prisoner

of wintry love walked in chill streets
past dormant gardens and discovering
roses in the snow.
Within their frozen globe they glowed
like suns, desire in ice.
You took them home.

Their golden blooms preserved immured
one perfect moment in this room.
I'll pick them now, my perfect gift
for you.

Though – what about the samovar,
the little flame you lit to brew our tea –
It was intended all along
for me.

THE SKATER

From the rising moon
a river of silver spilled between rocks,
through gullies, over the plateau,
        and travelling silently
splashed bony grasses, washed the living skeletons of trees,
scooped animals from their earths after kindling their eyes.
As it poured into beings their first moontime
it pooled in the brain of a newborn girl
where it crystallized,
and for twenty-seven years she went skating on it.

Beginning,
she wobbled, stumbled, slid,
        and proudly started over.
She glided and twirled and glissaded, matched to the surface
as her blades carved winged images of her in marble
        and unnoticed ancestors applauded,
until that brilliant day when, leaping free
and spinning through the air like a scimitar,
she saw beneath her that the ice was breaking up.

The pool of memory
and memory of light is pocked and grey and drifting
to pieces, channels opening in water
choppy as molars at a carrion feast.
She looks down at her lifelessness,
her skates still dancing in the air,
        her flight at its zenith,
and there in the dark and widening sea
surrounded by cruel waves and floes of slush
she sees them,
the astonishing beings, the swimmers
who are the ancestors struggling to save her marble images.

BLUE-EYED GRASS

Sisyrinchium

Tiny companions
for my walk are twinkling
from the roadside dust and weed.

As I chase
the sun-flung coins of thought
to gather up . . . they interrupt.

Six-petaled stars
distract where I'm waylaid
in spangles of wind-shaken shade.

I pursue the ancestors ahead
though leaves like tambourines are jangling
birdsong tangling as they disappear
around the bends of past. I seek
the careful clue, a honeyjar ant-scoured,
a fallen shoe, some gift whereby

I'd know their recollection that
they'd made this road for me.
But a perfection

of blue-flowering eyes is all
they show. I fancy giggles
follow me

of children merry in my track,
yet whirling back I just see
blue-eyed grass.

WRECKAGE

The man's parts
yawed across the lakebed
would have been her husband.
Even so, it was she who kept watch
beside the wreckage, the only mourner.

It could have been her husband if
either she had married this man
or the man she married were in this lake.
Even so, it was she
who vainly tried to pull
pieces of fuselage from the silt
as though to reconstruct her world
                    but they only sank deeper.

Loons considered her deluded,
pretending they could not locate her while
swimming overhead like search-and-rescue outboards.
A blue goose, northbound,
spotting the debris of broken secrets
was able to read her heart beneath the reflected moon.
Fishes driven off by the cataclysm
returned cautiously to feed
in their waters of dead possibilities.

Surfacing
she struck out toward the receding shore where
on an antler of gleaming driftwood she stuck
pink pebbles, a blue feather,
and her own shell-like fingernails
as a memorial to the neitherness of life
spent in deep cold
                    and freely left with the wreckage.

Like sunset then, followed by the wave of dark,
she crawled up the beach and flew away on the sky
watching the shadow flying under her
              grow huge across the tundra.
It would have been her shadow, right?

Whether so, she disappeared into it.

A THEORY OF EVOLUTION

In they bolt bewildered from the wide range
of the prairies laboriously fenced by their lifetimes.

She, summoning and circling and driving them on
like a winter storm cloud,
smiles to their naying from the corral
as the smell of singed hide reaches their nostrils,
as the ropes strain when she brands the select as hers.

If this is beginning to sound familiar
don't doubt your ears.
You know who I mean,
the wind who shakes the china tree 'til it shatters,
who rattles the stone chimes for entry,
this woman has plans.

The injuries she inflicts she will soothe until,
while snow sifts layers onto the sills
and drifts against the door,
you forget the sweetness of the wild ones you've abandoned.
Grass music is stoppered by the clink of silence.
You won't discern her house,
only the transposing patterns of broken light
as your legacy reels through the roof-hole
from the blaze of your sense.
When she holds a mirror to your blindness
she conceals its frame and her tell-tale fingertips
in fancies
and trims your excess and spuriousness to a new style
without you feeling the shears.

Be especially wary during lazy moments in the afternoon
to outrun the lasso of the telephone line.
And moreover beware your evening shower
is not so caustic as to wholly eat
the day you wear.
Then when at night you lie down with her,
believing your wide-ranging ruse is safe
within her fences of sleep,
check that the straw is not on fire.

SNOW STORIES

During two rotations past the starfields
through the gates of the sun
frost-shackled Earth can smell the breath of snow,
watch warning leaflets waft from shunting freight-clouds,
melt teasers on her tongue.
It arrives by stealth in a feather cloak,
whispering affection and shaking out season's greetings,
lulls and wraps soft with promises
and settles like sleep.
But rousing from its deception
it snarls round midnight
whipping wind cords, blasting ice frenzies
until its white work
              the trussed beauty
is presented on the catwalk of dawn.

*

Pretend numb astonishment, write mercilessly
of diamonds, of oblivion
and the tragedy of snow,
of snow
falling in forests where partisans
hide their broken causes and escape
in winter art snatched from fir boughs,
or deepening on switchback roads
to mountain villages
where it obliterates the secrets of a people,
or cowling the festive lights
which swing through winter-blinded streets
like seditious elves.

Snow lasts forever, as do dark ages.
Endeavours are dead leaves
nourishing Earth.

*

A storm piles onto the horizon,
black as a mediaeval fortress,
slits of sky glinting
like flames in a banquet hall,
arrows of sleet
stinging upturned innocent faces.
I retreat.
Curtain drawn back for the last daylight,
I observe the ground already surrendered in white.

I listen all night
and the next to my burial
hush, I pray,
arise from the dead and greet a figure
of snow, perhaps
a knot of itself in a whirl
or a shade of pine at the gate
who asks, Are you ready?

Prospect at peace, an ethereal gallery,
forgiven saints in radiant robes,
ironic lives commuted to alabaster:
the kingdom redeemed
by snow.
My coat's on a peg, my boots by the door,
I put them on, wind a scarf
and I go.

WISE WOMEN

Hastening by the jack pine
and down a slope of escaping phlox,
I catch in my lens
eye an oval council on a dais
moored in a lily bed on summer-grey water.
Three sunhats confer, confide
- palm-frond, coolie
and a printed linen from Annabel's Gift Emporium.

I am walking downhill
past the jack pine bent
with the character of the wind
in its years, while frolicking phlox
from an overflowing garden
challenges me to race my own time
to a seedy finish line.

As I go down to sun on the rocks
carrying a sketchbook for disguise,
I wear my cerise bathing suit from Annabel's
under a maternity shirt my daughter discarded.
The exclusive trio gracing the raft
are confessing their charms. Inadvertently
I embody all three spells of womanhood.

Like floating in glass I lack traction repeatedly
passing the haggard tree. Beyond rocks,
reedy shallows and the lapping water weed
the conference spins - no agenda,
just fateful powers of redirection.
Wisps of words and drifts of mirth
shatter the stillness of the day.

I study them like oracles.

Maybe I will
stumble across the spill of seed,
teeter on rocks, wade shallows,
swim the treacherous lily bed.
Three queens ride clouds across the afternoon
following a luminous evolution.
I'll offer to be their camel girl.

BLACK . . .

. . . crows
ragged tears in the fabric of the landscape
splits of space appearing hither and thither
in the yellow fields and woodland greenery
as though the gods are playing with boomerangs

. . . shirt
I've hung on a line to dry leaving
the garden colour undulating around
the shape of a hole in the wind

. . . horse
standing before bright water
still as iron
tail of splayed fire, sparks in its mane
wrought of an opening in the light

. . . silhouette
outlines of precious curly heads
cut with clever scissors at fairgrounds
to be found in old albums alongside funeral portraits
(though nowadays they snap your photo with the clown)

. . . eye patch
focusing the blindspot
whether on illusion's toys
        the forbidding future
                or a window into another universe,
some incredulous time will explore the darkness
as it once explored the black interiors of continents
which yielded their wild-eyed men
                to the discovery of wild-eyed men.

50

TIME ZONE

Here you come
ticking into the particular
from possibility,
setting your pulse as you start
the climb up the sand staircase
in a shifting desert

watched only
by five marionettes of papier mache
perched on a rail fence ever
waiting to dance
to a clockwork band
I wind myself with a key
cut from a lodestone at the entrance.

Music - harmonica, banjo,
one-string bass -
trails from your thought
caught
in a tree like a kite
or a hanged man
- your choice, the iconography -
which you free in time.

          In time
the scudding kite
the swinging man
will undo crime, will fight the wind,
and you will journey down
the way you came
through memory
on crumbled stairs in drifted sands
past marionettes, five
soaked to their shoulders
in the wadi.

Their glass eyes glinting never move,
yet follow as you flounder by.
The band is strumming idly
as they make their last request:
After you run out of time
do not forget to close the door behind you
please . . .

TWO CHAIRS

(from *Gifts from the Dead*)

The kitchen chairs
with wooden ladder backs plained by time
are near the door outside
where I was sitting on the one with the calico cushion
in the sun, shelling beans I'd dried.

You climbed upon the other
from where you watched
the dragons in the purple forest hover.
There,
          you pointed as one with fire-spun wings
approached your brown knees. It circled
and came in to land.
Out flew your hand, which stalled, and then
you stared into the creature's eyes
          glittering with messages,
puzzled at its mouth moving in silent language
- presages, so it seemed,
          from a world we couldn't imagine -
admired its handsome suit of turquoise mail
belted with carnelian, unidentifiable honours
awarded to an alien.

After the dragonfly darted away again to the asters,
you came in to play and I to cook, and now
a quiet rain falls. Through the screen I look
at the forgotten chairs: forlorn,
proud and patient they stretch their backs, scanning
for our royal visitor's return.

OWL

(from *Gifts from the Dead*)

Air reduced to form,
   spectral
owl traverses layers and lengths of light,
the complexes of a parallel territory,
   assured seeker
riding currents of alter-awareness.

Hungering hunter
   on a broken tree,
      disciplined
she is still as a mounted trophy
until   swivelling her head
in an instant she takes charge
   of three-quarters of the universe.

Through colonnades and catacombs
of a woodlot
two boys stalk squirrels,
spending the free coinage of morning
as if it really did grow on the aspens,
crossing the field at noon
in the silvery heat.
One climbs the rail fence
to the house on the edge of town,
disappearing inside
as the screen door bangs.
The other stops before the fence,
   outside
   always outside
as though locked out of this dimension
and cannot disappear
   even into arms of kindness.

Rapt
he remains there
gazing at a raptor,
    the owl
who gazes at him
        like a human moon.
Her wings open
in a great cloak
    scalloped with the sun's flares,
and she descends,
a long glide of darkness growing
eclipsing the aureole of sky,
        paralyses the boy in her talons,
            pinions him with her feathers,
softly folds him to her downy heart.

MEDITATIONS IN WOODLAND

An interior
of halls and mysteries
the columns and arches of trees
structure a sanctuary
of green.

I and I,
vanishing down infinite aisles,
are trees, initiates graced
through the clerestory
with messages from the sun.

Time takes root in us
and slows its breath circling itself
with ring on ring and wearing
one by one the garments of the seasons:
bird-threaded spring song through lace,
green-patterned green
                              on green,
an older wilder time in fiery scarves,
and coldly sequined, a remembrance
replacing the leaves
in the clarity of a frost-stilled night.

Searching the lake as if
to find my face
among those in a photograph
                              I only see
that I and I and I are trees
the lake reflects.

I watch you come traipsing
to lure me back to you
                    to me
and turn away unseeing
so well in time
can clothes confer identity.
Once so, for your bewilderment
I leave you herbs. I leave
them at the roadside, taking
your dust for transmutation.
Go now, with care,
                    for I
and I may not become myself again.

TWO GERANIUMS

in a white flowerpot
are coloured inkpen red
                          on a blue noon,
two nosegays
                          presented to each other
            like a pair of projected lovers.

Beneath the fans of foliage,
where ants gnaw the carcasses of microbes
and spiders swing down the revolutionary vine system
they extrude into the dusky gnat-whipped air,
a beetle in shining armour tilts
                          on a lump of garden soil

to dazzle the fluters unseen in the galleries,
the painters of sunrises on the leaves
rigged like skies among vast towering stems
of his scented rainforest . . .

Merely, though, fancies created by his eye centre
to explain mystery
                    for
                          descending through the canopy
a winged golden messenger from the land of honey
buzzes word of the king and queen
                          blooming in an incredible heaven.

PIDGINS

popcorn   rush   queue up   queue up
push pass peck   stuff stuff   tough fluff
need seed   feed need   oops goop
swoop snoop coo   rap whoop   clack

promenade across the tiles
puffing plumage   fanning flight
boss   swell   doss   dwell
up a wall and down on ledge
strut   flap   trap a lady
roost in roof   fuss and fledge

steal the spills from picnic baskets
pick specks from paths   from benches snack bits
sham for handouts from panhandlers
once come night   caves light
warm a shadow safe and tight
tuck us in   sleep   cheap
cliffs fair-shared   home   lends
to flocks of our unfeathered friends

MY GREAT GRANDMOTHER'S WEDDING SHOES

are almost small enough for your feet
I said to my granddaughter, look
white satin, and these little bows.

Satin rainbows, she said, I see rainbows.

Thin dainty slippers carried her up the cold stone aisle
of the church to be married.

Carried her over the bridge of her dreams in style,
sighed my granddaughter.

The minister told them their duties and made them vow
to be true, and then my great grandfather
gave his bride a ring and a kiss.

Did she kiss him too? asked the child.

Afterwards tea and cake
perhaps in the garden if the day were fine.

No, no, they drank pink wine and played with balloons
   - the girl was sashaying round the room -
and they danced through the night by the light of the moo-oo-oon.

I shook my head. Dear, there in that day
wine and dance were forbidden. So they would pray
for they thought God was stern.

If they had kept quiet, God couldn't learn of it.
Did God forbid her to throw her bouquet
when the cake was all gone and they were driving away
in your great grandfather's car with the top down?

With a mocking frown I tried to explain,
Dear, there were no cars.

Weren't they allowed either?

No, just not invented. They went to the seaside by train.
She changed her shoes though because of the soot -

And no doubt the rain, the child muttered.
Did she tell you all this? I think you lied.

I never knew her.
One year before I was born she died.

Promise you won't do that to *my* daughter -
How stern was the way this granddaughter eyed me.

PATCHWORK PASTORAL

Seven black cows in a mint-green field,
Five sheep drowsing by a pink rock,
Three golden gulls
Round the rollicking sun.
Six lucky heather sprays stitched onto a hill,
Four cloud gardens in silver and grey,
Two lace waterfalls.
One glad rainstorm, three lost lakes,
Five smoke skeins over seven richmen's roofs,
And nine warm breadloaves.
Eight hungering, six blessed, four parting, two friends,
                    One love . . .

Seven mint cows and five pink sheep,
Three glad gulls in the skein of the sun,
Six lacy heather sprays, four black clouds,
Two silver waterfalls stitched on a hill.
One parting rainstorm, three gold lakes,
Five grey smokerings over seven friendly richmen,
And nine blessed breadloaves in a green garden.
Seven lucky, five lost, three rollicking, one love . . .

Seven hungry cows,
Five blessed sheep,
And three friendly gulls
In the pink sun.
Six skeins of heather,
Four parting clouds,
Two golden waterfalls sprayed over the rock.
One silver rain rollicking on the roof,
Three lace lakes stitched round a hill,
Five smoke gardens in black and grey,
Seven lucky richmen in a mint field,
And nine lost breadloaves.
Ten glad, eight drowsy, six greening, four stormy, two warm,
                    One love . . .

ISLAND IN THE MIDDLE OF THE NIGHT

At an unearthly hour closed
within starry black sleep
I am bell-roused
to some bright silent country
I always thought mythical

but a real driver at the door ready
to conduct me with his dashboard dials
through a night surrounding
the continuously fleeing arc of headlights

is to drop me into the humming machinery
of an airport
self-contained as a planet
abiding by its own peculiar laws

from which I am airborne into dawn
glimpsed through bubble-wrap
lowered again
like Icarus in a shopping bag
at the entrusted destination.

The handles of lateral connection
break, and I am left
hanging by the rays of the sun
in a sparkling dark sea.

LAST QUARTER

The signal is seen at daybreak
near the zenith
 a fading lantern left glowing
provisional
 utilitarian
misshapen by a hurried tinsmith before he disappeared with
 his dark
 his impatient mistress.

I want to linger in one doorway or another for the sun
to find, seduce me, hold me longer.

Yet there are signs:
glasses of October wine, ruby, amber,
 left half-drunk by (almost) empty chairs
or on the table disarrayed
 around a dying centrepiece,
the tide half out and racing
 to its assignation
 in the arms of the horizon
 abandoning aphrodisiac on the half shell.

 I can't wait around for
my oyster to return some April noon what with

summer to fold away in timelock
and the chairs to tilt against the rain
 at an angle fatalistic as it is unusable,
the dead flower piece to be cast into the sea
with my message for the fish - my dread
 foretells I'll see it once again
 when torn and bobbing -

So what remains
of those who set their glasses down
and vanished into laughter?

Their ambered or their rubied lips
        which kiss goodbye
                        like butterflies

            in light distraction

    each with one   and with another

        before the time
                        unseen
                                unmissed
    the moon's last quarter

                    sets.

BRICK WALL WITH APPLE BLOSSOM

A veil of light
shining with spring rain the blossoms
overhang the slick red wall
steadfast with geometry,
cultivation for the fickle beauty
of the captive tree.

A dancer or a bride, you think,
revelling in radiance unconcealed
from her interpreters
who envy joy or admire insouciance
the way readers of a golden text
construe its message.

Down the road
from the red brick church troop mourners
dressed like ravens whose lament
lasts in the wrap of damp air
as long as yew wreaths.
The ravaged bough above
is scattering petals in mimed heartbreak.

Does the man following the hearse
behold the white cloud
of his dead wife's hair? No,
you've heard, this is
the funeral of his son
                    shot by an avenger.

It would have been his wedding.

Glancing up
the anguished father sees the ghosts
of Romeo and Juliet
entwined in satin.

Lightning Source UK Ltd.
Milton Keynes UK
01 February 2011

166722UK00001B/36/P

9 781906 628086